D1742404

RIVERS AND CANALS

PENNY MARSHALL

Macdonald

Jacket pictures

Front(main): At the stern of a narrow boat, Grand Union Canal
Front(small): Tower Beach, River Thames, London
Back(top): Restoration work on the Stroudwater Canal, Gloucestershire
Back(bottom): A traditional skill – using rope to make 'torpedo' protection
   bolsters for boats

A MACDONALD BOOK

First published in 1986 by
Macdonald & Co. (Publishers) Ltd
London and Sydney

© Macdonald & Co. (Publishers) Ltd 1986

ISBN 0 356 11394 9

Macdonald & Co (Publishers) Ltd
Greater London House
Hampstead Road
London NW1 7QX

A BPCC PLC company

Printed by Purnell & Sons (Book Production) Ltd
Paulton, near Bristol, Avon

All rights reserved

BRITISH LIBRARY CATALOGUING IN PUBLICATION DATA

Marshall, Penny
   Rivers and canals.–(The Camera as witness; 8)
   1. Inland navigation–Great Britain–History
   –Juvenile literature
   I. Title   II. Series
   386'.0941   HE663

ISBN 0-356-11394-9

CREDITS

Abbot Hall Art Gallery, Kendal:
   18(top)
Barnaby's: front cover(main), 4,
   37(bottom), 38, 39, 40(top)
BBC Hulton Picture Library: 6,
   9(bottom), 29
Bodleian Library: 8(bottom)
BPCC: 5
British Waterways Board: back
   cover bottom), title page, 22-23,
   22(bottom), 24, 25, 26, 27, 28, 34,
   36, 37(top), 40-41 Hugh McKnight
London Borough of Hounslow: 19(top)
Howarth-Loomes Collection: 7(top),
   7(centre), 7(bottom), 8(top), 13,
   21(top)
Lambeth Archives: 9(top)
Manchester Public Libraries: 14-15,
   15(top), 30, 35(top)
Mansell Collection: 12, 14(top), 18-19,
   35(bottom)
National Monuments Record: 11
Norfolk Museums Service: 20
Norwich Central Library: 21(bottom)
Oxfordshire County Libraries: 16, 17
Derek Pratt: back cover(top), 41(top),
   42, 43(left), 43(right), 44(top),
   44(bottom)
Royal Institution of Cornwall: 10
Topham: front cover (inset), 31, 32,
   33(top), 33(bottom)

Picture research by Diana Morris

Contents

Introduction

Rivers, wherever they are, have provided food, transport and work for the people who live by them for as long as there have been people. But rivers are natural waterways and so may be unreliable. The amount of water in them varies according to the time of year, they may flow too fast, too slowly or be too rocky or too shallow for use. In other words, rivers are not always easy to control. Canals, on the other hand, are completely artificial and so quite controllable. Once built they provide few unexpected surprises.

In 1857, when the earliest photograph in this book was taken, canals had been an essential part of Britain's transport system for nearly 100 years. In fact, without canals to provide cheap reliable transport for both raw materials and finished goods, the Industrial Revolution of the late eighteenth and early nineteenth centuries would have been almost impossible. Certainly

rivers were used for this transport too, but rivers follow routes dictated by the geography of a country, not the economics of an industry. And though canals were immensely expensive to build, the country's increasing population and rapid industrialization brought great wealth to many of those involved in their development.

The coming of the railways in the nineteenth century was the beginning of the end of the canals. At first it seemed that canals and railways could co-exist – the early steam engines were unreliable and could not travel very long distances. But that quickly changed. The network of railways soon extended all over Britain, engines became bigger, faster and more reliable, so they could pull heavier trains that reached their destinations more quickly.

In the face of this competition the decline of water-borne traffic was inevitable. Bigger, more powerful

boats could be used on rivers, but this was impossible on the narrow canals, where the 'wash' created by powerful engines would quickly have destroyed the canal banks.

Commercial cargo traffic on British canals ceased in 1970. Ironically, the last cargoes were the same as those which had started the whole canal industry over 200 years earlier: coal.

But both canals and rivers have now taken on a new lease of life. As sources of recreation and leisure activities, they offer far more attractive possibilities than disused railways or roads can ever do!

(Below) A pair of narrow boats go through a lock on the Grand Junction Canal near Berkhampstead, Hertfordshire, 1950s. Such a scene would have been familiar to any of the canal people you will meet in this book.

HOW TO USE THIS BOOK

The photos in this book give a good idea of both the prosperity and the decline of Britain's waterways in the last century and a quarter. They also show how little some things have changed.

As you read through the book, look out for the things that are different from today, and for things that are the same. You can tell, too, from people's expressions what they are thinking, and that certainly hasn't changed!

Learn to look closely at the photographs, and to draw conclusions from what you see. Although they were never intended as such, all the photographs in this book are important documents in our social history.

The date at the top of each page tells you when the photograph was taken.

A NOTE ABOUT PHOTOGRAPHY

In the 1850s, when this book starts, photography was very much a new and unusual hobby, a pastime for a few scientifically-minded amateurs with servants to carry the heavy, cumbersome equipment. Taking photographs was a laborious process. The sitter had to stay still for several minutes while the image was exposed on the photographic plate. Any movement, however slight, would come out as a blur.

Early photographs were processed onto metal and glass as well as paper. Improvements came first through the experiments of individuals, usually working alone to solve problems. Early great pioneers included William Henry Fox Talbot, Frederick Scott Archer and the Frenchman, Louis Daguerre. Their discoveries helped to make photography what it is today.

With today's cameras it is possible for anyone to take a photo – just point the camera and snap! But that hasn't reduced photography's important role as a recorder of history – the history of individuals as well as great events. Every photograph, however ordinary, can be considered an historical document. As you will discover in this book, there's a lot you can learn from a photograph!

The photograph below was taken in 1907. Cameras were already much simpler than in the very early days of photography, but were still slow and difficult to use.

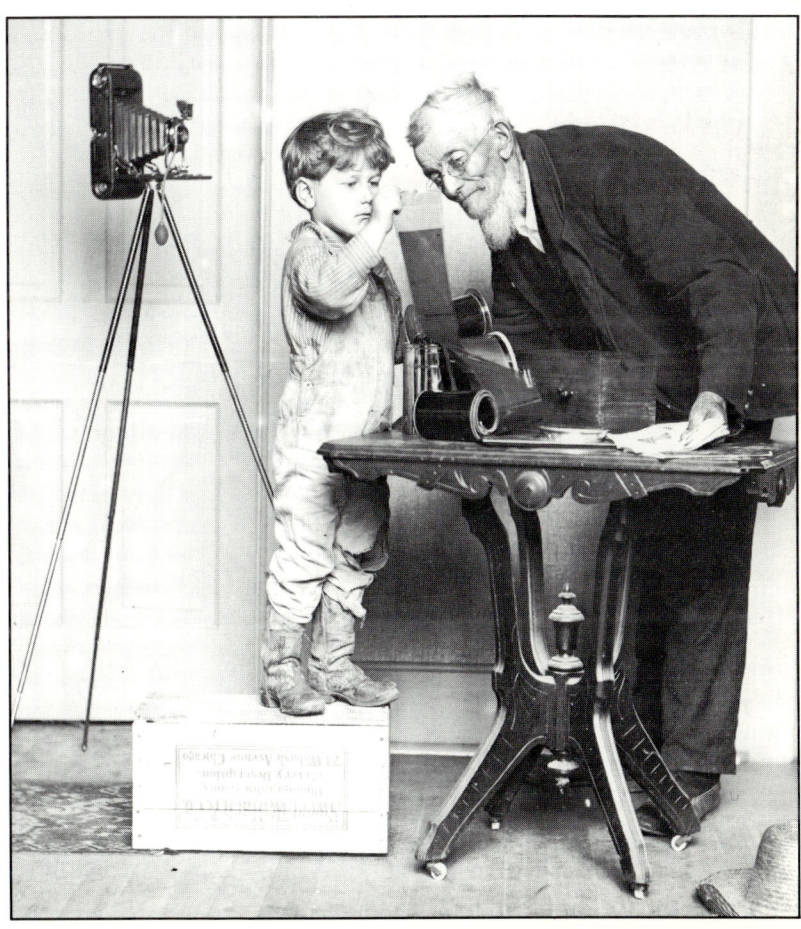

TWO MEN FISHING

The stillness of the water suggests that these two men have chosen an ideal day for fishing. They have tucked their punt into the bank, cast their line and are now hoping for a bite.

The rod looks rather short and clumsy compared with today's long slim ones, but then this photograph was taken in 1857. The photographer, William Grundy, took many pictures of the English countryside which he published as 'Views of England'.

Look at the beautifully woven fishing basket, or creel, which you can see almost as well reflected in the water. Notice, too, the men's clothes. The one standing up is wearing a smock over his shirt and breeches. These were the working clothes of every countryman at this time. The style of the smock changed slightly from area to area, but that was all.

The other man wears a close-fitting jacket – you can see that it's wrinkled or pulling a little under the arm – and pale close-fitting trousers. These clothes, and his black high crowned hat suggest that he is no farmworker. Perhaps he's one of the gentry being given a fishing lesson by the local gamekeeper.

EASING CONGESTION

Traffic in cities was a problem even in Victorian times, and it was particularly bad in London. A solution to London's problem was proposed in 1862: the north bank of the Thames would be built up and strengthened so that a road could go along it – the Embankment, as it is still called. Work began in 1864 and was completed in 1870.

The photograph below shows one of the first piles to be put in position at the start of the work. In the background is Waterloo Bridge.

LONDON WHARFS

(Above) You won't find a postcard of London like this today, although this was the equivalent 130 years ago. The view of St Paul's Cathedral was taken from Southwark Bridge as one of a series of stereographic views of London. (Stereographs were a very early type of photograph.)

Look at the warehouses crowding down to the water's edge, and the barges moored alongside, waiting to be loaded or unloaded. Just in front of White's warehouse are two sailing barges. You can see their masts and dark furled sails.

The crowded wharfs indicate the importance and prosperity of Britain's waterways. In 1845 over 4 million tonnes of goods were transported on the Birmingham Canal Navigations. And 68,000 narrow boats that year went into Birmingham or took goods out. But competition from the railways was increasing, and the canal age was being relentlessly replaced by the age of railways.

FLOODING IN THE FENS

Most of the great engineering works of the canal age were completed before photography had been invented. However, this photograph (left), taken in 1862, shows one rather unusual engineering project.

The dam controls the water draining from reclaimed land into the drainage canals across the Middle Level of the Fens, at Whittlesey Mere near Peterborough. The amount of water pouring through the raised sluice gates suggests that there has been bad flooding.

The men in the tall hats are the contractor who built the dam and the engineers who designed it. They look quite confident that the dam will withstand the pressure of the floodwater.

A PEACEFUL SCENE

This peaceful scene on the River Wye at Hereford (that's Hereford Cathedral in the background) seems to suggest that the railways had already overwhelmed the waterways in the competition for cargo.

That was not yet true when this picture was taken in the 1860s, although some of the smaller canals were in difficulties and many went out of business in the 1870s. However, what the photograph really indicates is the problem of using some rivers for transport.

The Wye was a particularly difficult river for navigation. It was liable to flooding, and there were rapids which it was not easy to get a boat over. In fact, once the Newport, Abergavenny and Hereford Railway opened in 1854, the river was rarely used.

A quiet row in one of the skiffs this boatman has for hire was a pleasant way to spend a sunny afternoon for those with time to spare. And that was about the only traffic that used the river.

FOLLY BRIDGE

Look at these boys fishing. They may not be wearing jeans and tee-shirts, but the attractions of water and fishing are as irresistible as they have probably always been.

In the background of the photograph are Salter's boatyard and Folly Bridge, both famous Oxford landmarks (see also page 17).

On the left, just beyond the boys, is a pair of lock gates. These lead into a navigable stretch of river. You can see someone standing on the loading platform that juts out from the second storey windows of the warehouse. Perhaps there is a boat approaching loaded with cargo.

FROZEN IN

(Right) If you earned your living working on the rivers or canals, a harsh winter such as that of 1887 could be disastrous.

These barges are frozen in beside the Thames at Putney – near the starting point of the annual Oxford and Cambridge boat race. From the bleakness of the scene and the piled up ice and snow, it looks as if it will be many days before the barges will be able again to make their way up or down river on the tide.

Meanwhile there is nothing the bargees can do except wait. The boy leaning against the tiller of barge No. 633, registered at Lambeth, could be the son of the man who worked the barge. Although he doesn't look very old, he's almost certainly not on holiday from school, or even playing truant. In 1887, when this photograph was taken, the school leaving age was only 13, and that wasn't strictly enforced. In fact, providing barge children with any sort of education was quite a problem – see pages 27 and 32.

A THAMES BARGE

(Left) Here, with Richmond Bridge in the background, is a closer view of a Thames barge. Compare it with the one at the top of page 7. You can see the mast, the rigging and the dark shape of the rolled up sail very clearly.

These barges were really rather clumsy vessels. They were built to carry cargo – not for speed. To help make them more manoeuvrable they were fitted with lee-boards. These boards were fixed about halfway along each side – you can see the one nearest the camera – and could be raised or lowered as required to help steer the boat.

KING HARRY'S FERRY

Rivers may help transport and communications, but they can also be a barrier. Bridges are the obvious solution, and bridges have been built for thousands of years, but it is only in the last 100 years or so that it has been possible to bridge very wide rivers. Before that, ferries were used instead.

This photograph shows the King Harry ferry across the River Fal in Cornwall. From it you can tell that ferries were often far from convenient. First the horse had to be unhitched from the carriage and led on board the ferry – not always easy with a spirited or nervous horse.

Then the carriage or cart had to be dragged on board. This, too, was quite difficult. Even passenger carriages were heavy, and the planks on to the ferry were dangerously narrow – at least, if this photograph is anything to go by. Then the passengers went on, and the ferryman rowed or poled the ferry across to the other side of the river.

Once there, the process was reversed. Everything was taken off the ferry, the horses were reharnessed to the carriages, and the travellers continued on their way. Though inconvenient, however, ferry crossings generally saved a

very long journey to the nearest bridge.

The two ladies on this ferry are going to find it difficult to keep the hems of their dresses clear of the mud. But, as a precaution against this sort of thing, the hems are probably edged with braid or a fringe, so that it is these which will get dirty and not the material of the dress. In the days before dry-cleaning and synthetic fabrics, replacing trimmings was one way to keep a dress looking smart.

BUILDING TOWER BRIDGE

This, of course, is the other way to cross a river! And what a contrast it will be to the country ferry opposite!

This striking photograph was taken probably in 1889, during the very early stages of the building of Tower Bridge in London. The bridge's basic steel frame is clearly visible as it rises above the traffic on the river and the warehouses on each bank. Compare its structure with that of Waterloo Bridge visible in the background of the righthand photo on page 7.

Notice, too, the difference in the boats in this view of the River Thames compared with those at the top of page 7. That photograph was taken in about the same place as this one, yet what a change there has been in shipping since then. There were no steam ships in that photograph, while in this one there don't seem to be any sailing vessels at all.

A pair of barges, or lighters, are moored in midstream and there are many more tied up near the bank. They are too big to go on canals, but once loaded they will probably be towed in groups downstream to the mouth of the Thames. If they are taken upstream any cargoes bound for the canals or upper reaches of the Thames will have to be transferred into smaller boats to complete the journey.

11

HENLEY REGATTA

(Left) What a contrast this photograph is with the others so far in this book. It shows a completely different aspect of rivers in Victorian Britain.

This marvellous photograph of Henley Royal Regatta was taken in 1893 by Henry Taunt (see below). Henley, as it was generally known, was one of the high points of 'the Season', that round of social events attended by all who considered themselves fashionable.

Racing is over for the day and now it is time for the spectators to take to the river and try their skill. What an array of boats there is: punts, skiffs, dinghies and even a canoe. There's a party going on in the boat with the striped awning – perhaps they are celebrating winning a race.

Look at the clothes these people are wearing: the men with their blazers, boaters and rowing club caps, and the women in dresses with long skirts and fashionably tight bodices. Of course, they were used to such clothes, but keeping clean and elegant in a boat on the river must have been quite difficult.

HENRY TAUNT

(Below) The structure on the top of his cabin leaves no doubt about how Henry Taunt earns his living! Nor, when you look at his transport, is it surprising that he was able to take that marvellous photograph of Henley (left).

According to his signboard, he works in Oxford. That's probably one reason why he uses a boat – Oxford, like Cambridge, has a university where for over a century rowing has been one of the chief sporting activities. So any photographer who used a boat was sure of getting good pictures of the many races held each year.

MANCHESTER SHIP CANAL

Throughout the nineteenth century the industrialization of Britain continued fast. The north-west, and particularly Liverpool, thrived as trade with the USA developed.

The industrialists of Manchester, the centre of the country's cotton trade, looked enviously at Liverpool's port. Manchester, an inland city, had nothing similar, and so was at a disadvantage.

But Manchester had a well-deserved reputation for imagination and enterprise. The city might not be on the sea, but the sea could be brought to it. And so the Manchester Ship Canal was built. It was officially opened in May 1894, and for the first time enabled large ocean vessels to reach the city.

The picture at the top of the page shows sailing ships on the canal at Saltport. Beside the nearest one is a steam tug and one of the local 'flats', wide shallow barges used to carry heavy cargoes. On the right bank, railway sidings enable goods trains to come close to the ships for easier loading and unloading.

The picture below shows steam-powered vessels at the wharfs, and a number of loaded barges. The barges are particularly interesting: on the sterns of three of them are the words 'Manchester Ship Canal Company Bridgewater Canals'.

In fact, it was the canal built by the Duke of Bridgewater, to carry coal from his mines at Worsley to the markets of Manchester, that first made people in Britain realize the possibility of canals as a practical means of transport. That canal, opened in 1761, was nearly 140 years old when this photograph was taken.

The Bridgewater Canal is little used now, except for pleasure boating, but the Manchester Ship Canal continues to play an important part in the commercial life of the north-west.

GRAND OPENING

(Above) With its freshly painted twin funnels, or smoke stacks, and pennants flying in the stiff breeze, the *SS Hotspur* goes down the Manchester Ship Canal to mark the opening of the canal in 1894. Perhaps it's just the angle from which the photograph was taken, but the *Hotspur* looks very lop-sided with its load of local dignitaries.

Watching from the bank are the people from the nearby houses, who must have followed the progress of the canal as it was built.

Notice that the *Hotspur* is a paddle steamer, not a type of boat that was ever very common in Britain. In the days before steam, most areas of the country had their own distinctive types of boat. These types had evolved over the years and reflected the conditions of the local river and the cargoes the boats had to carry. The coming of steam, a source of power which for the first time made boats independent of wind and tide, led to the gradual decline of the local types of boat.

THE COALYARD

Clearly it is a special day at Frank Restall's coalyard beside the Oxford Canal – the photographer has come (still something of a novelty).

All the normal everyday bustle and activity has stopped. Everything has been beautifully set out, from the carts and loaded wheelbarrows down to the nets in the foreground filled with hay for the horses. Even the piles of coal (look at the size of some of the lumps!) seem remarkably neat and tidy.

The people, too, look rather still and unnatural. This is probably because they were standing still for the photographer. Film was 'slower' then than it is now, which meant that the image being photographed took longer to register on the film. If anyone moved while the photograph was being taken, it showed as a blur on the final picture (one of the ferrymen on page 10 is blurred for this reason). As this picture is clearly intended to be an 'official' company photograph, no-one wanted to move and spoil it.

Do you think that's Frank Restall standing in the front with his wife just behind? And what about the older man behind her? Perhaps *he's* the Frank Restall who founded the business, and it's his son in the foreground who now runs it.

On the left of the photograph are the narrow boats which bring the coal to this wharf in Hayfield Road, Oxford. They, too, look surprisingly clean for vessels that carry coal. Down each side run the canvas sheets which were used to cover the cargo. You can see some of them in position on the first narrow boat.

And look at the clothes of the boat women. How did they ever manage to keep their aprons and magnificent bonnets so white?

LIFEBOAT SATURDAY

Taken in Oxford in 1900, a few years after the photograph opposite, this picture shows a very different side of the city.

Most of these men in their straw boaters (can you spot the woman wearing a boater?) were probably quite unaware of Frank Restall and the canal people who came to Hayfield Wharf. He may have supplied coal to some of their colleges, but that was not their concern. They were at Oxford to enjoy themselves and to study – and for many of them it was in that order, too.

The photograph was taken during Lifeboat Saturday, in June 1900. The lifeboat, manned by the Southend lifeboat crew, was brought upriver to Oxford to be the centrepiece of a special fund-raising event for the RNLI (Royal National Lifeboat Institution).

Here at Salter's boatyard by Folly Bridge (see also page 8), in a city famous for its rowing on the river, large crowds have gathered to watch the boat being launched for demonstrations of its work at sea. Spectators have climbed lampposts and are thronging windows to get a better view.

Some have also taken to punts – Oxford's traditional river pleasure boat. And just beyond the *City of London* there's a band, waiting to head a special procession around the city. How splendid it was to have some fun – *and* support a charity!

Rivers are not just a means of transport or an excuse for a day out. Far upstream, where they are too narrow for cargo-carrying boats and too fast for pleasure boating, they are used by the people who live near them in ways that have changed little over many centuries.

Both the pictures on this page were taken at the turn of the century and show traditional ways people used their local rivers.

SHEEP DIPPING

Many insects find the long fleeces of sheep ideal places in which to lay their eggs, which can harm both the sheep and the fleece. There are pesticides to deal with this problem now, but before they were invented, washing the sheep was the only solution.

Farmers used natural ponds, or diverted upland rivers to form pools, in which to wash the sheep.

This photograph, taken in Rydal, Westmoreland, at the beginning of this century, suggests that washing sheep was easier said than done. Though sheep can swim, they don't like water, and it will take two men to get this handsome, curly-horned ram into the pond. The man with the piece of wood is there to make sure that the sheep do not get out before their coats are thoroughly wet.

CORACLES

(Right) The coracles in which these men are going fishing were made by stretching skins over a framework of reeds. Coracles have been used on Welsh rivers for hundreds of years. The clothes worn by the coracle fishermen have changed, but their boats hardly at all.

Notice here how each man holds the single paddle between his first and second fingers and supports it against his arm. This ensures that he has one hand free to deal with the fishing line or nets.

The photograph was taken near Cenarth in Dyfed.

THE FERRYMAN

Mr Simmons (above) stands proudly in his boat, holding an oar – the symbol of his job as ferryman. For forty years he took foot passengers across the River Thames at Church Ferry, Isleworth, on the western edge of London. (If you ever visit Kew Gardens look for signs to the Brentford Gate. That is where Mr Simmons took his passengers to and from.)

In the days before bridges could be built across wide rivers, the job of ferryman was an important one, and it often stayed in one family, passing from father to son.

Look at Mr Simmons's hands and then compare them with your father's. Unless he does a lot of heavy work, his hands probably won't be nearly as large as Mr Simmons's. It's not surprising really – forty years of rowing a heavy boat across the Thames many times a day, whatever the weather and state of the tide, makes for big powerful hands, and muscles, too! 19

A FAMILY CRUISE

Cruising on the Norfolk Broads is nothing new, whatever the holiday brochures may suggest. And if the children's thick clothes and the billowing ensign at the stern are anything to go by, holiday weather was no better around 1900 than it is today.

The boat is a very fine motor launch – even if it is called *Terrible*. Look at the polished cabin roof, the brass work, the winch for lowering the bow anchor, and the cushioned seats for the passengers. The portholes suggest that there is plenty of cabin space should the weather turn really nasty.

The two girls are wearing sailor hats with *Terrible* written across the hat-bands – just like proper sailors. And do you think that is father standing proudly at the wheel, even though the boat is moored firmly to the bank?

In the background is a windmill, one of the many that dotted the area. They were essential for draining water from the land into the broads and other waterways. Without them the farmland first reclaimed in the seventeenth century would once again become a waterlogged and useless marshy fen.

EEL TRAPPING

(Right) A quite different view of the fens and broads of East Anglia is given by this photograph, taken in Norfolk about 1900. This couple will never know the luxury of being able to hire a boat for pleasure. For them the waterways provide a living, and in winter not a very good living at that.

Compare the clothes they are wearing with those of the people above. Even the uniforms worn by the crew on the ferry in Fort Augustus (opposite, top) look of better quality.

The woman's pinched face and bent shoulders are the result of a hard life and poor food, not just

FORT AUGUSTUS

(Right) These holidaymakers are disembarking at Fort Augustus near Inverness after an excursion on the Caledonian Canal, 1904. Notice how they are using the slatted cover of the paddle wheel as steps.

But how will the ladies manage when they want to get off the boat? There's a crew member to help them – he's standing with one foot on the shore and the other on the boat. He has just helped another passenger off. But that passenger was a man, wearing trousers and a short coat. It will not be as easy for these ladies, with their long skirts, hats, shawls and handbags, when it comes to that final jump on to the quayside!

concentration on her fishing line. Her husband is setting an eel trap. He has probably woven it himself from the willows that grow beside the water.

Notice how broad and shallow their boat is. This means it can float even in very little water – and some of the smaller streams were extremely shallow, clogged with water plants and silt left by the slow-flowing water.

In the background is the boathouse. It is made of branches, and thatched with the reeds that grow abundantly in the area. The couple's own simple home is probably also thatched with reeds.

1905

BARGE FAMILIES

The water of the canal across which these four narrow boats are moored is so still that you can see the families and their boats almost as clearly upside down in the reflection – even the decorated cabin doors and the painted watercans!

Only the lefthand boat is a steamer, the others have to be towed. The two central boats belong to different companies – Nelson, and Griffiths; so perhaps the steamer towed the *Edward VII* as its 'butty', and the other two worked together.

Notice how much higher the cabin of the steamer is compared with the cabins of the other three boats. This is to allow room for the engine, boiler and fuel store.

Notice, too, the different types of tiller bar used for steering. They're all painted in stripes, but the steamer has a metal one, like the one in the picture below, while the others have wooden ones. The wooden bars were used for more than just steering. Taken out of their sockets they could push the boat clear of the bank, drag the boat nearer the bank, clear anything fouling the tow-rope or even, in extreme cases, serve as a handy weapon in a fight!

Only one of the women is wearing the black bonnet which came into fashion among canal women after 1901. It was first worn as a gesture of mourning on the death of Queen Victoria, and remained popular for many years. Made of heavy cotton and lined with waterproof material, it provided a little protection against the weather.

The man on the left wears his narrow brimmed hat at a very jaunty angle. His waistcoat is similar to the one in the photograph on the right.

TWO MEN ON A NARROW BOAT

(Left) These two young men, eyeing the photographer rather warily, work for Fellows, Morton & Clayton, one of the best-known canal boat companies in the early part of this century.

The company, which was based in the Midlands, was also one of the few to provide its staff with uniforms. As you can see from the photograph, this followed what had become the canal boatmen's traditional wear – shirt with full sleeves, sleeveless waistcoat with brass buttons and velvet collar, wide leather belt and corduroy trousers held up with braided braces. A flat cap and neckerchief completed the everyday uniform. The jacket, similar to

the waistcoat but with long sleeves, was generally kept for 'best'.

Fellows, Morton & Clayton also took a pride in their boats. Look at the way these ones are decorated, with roses and scenic views painted on each side of the entrance to the cabins. This style of decoration, and the designs on the watercans on the cabin roofs, were to become much imitated, but there's nothing phoney about them here. These men and their dog were photographed at the turn of the century, long before such things became 'antiques'.

The chimney on the left shows that the nearest boat is steampowered. The small gadget on the

right of the chimney is the steam whistle. Steam-powered boats gave a smoother, faster ride than the more usual horse-drawn boats. But they had disadvantages. They needed a crew of three or four, instead of the two for horse boats.

Even more important, however, the engine and boiler took up a lot of valuable cargo space. Fellows, Morton & Clayton overcame this problem by specializing in the transport of expensive, high quality cargoes.

LOCK MAINTENANCE

It wasn't often that boat people saw a lock like this! But, like most other things, locks need regular maintenance and repair. This photograph of Hanwell Lock on the Grand Union Canal in Oxfordshire was taken in 1909 and shows very clearly how a lock was built – and also how narrow many of them were.

Although locks varied slightly in size from canal to canal, measurements of 22 metres long by 2 metres wide were fairly standard. With narrow boats not much smaller than the locks, getting the boats in and out was quite a tricky manoeuvre, and it's not surprising that legs or arms

were frequently crushed between the sides of the boat and the lock.

Locks were heavy to operate, particularly for the women and children who had to work them while their husbands or fathers were getting the boat in. But without locks there would have been no canals, for locks enable canals to cross country that is not flat.

Some of the systems of locks built in the great days of canal building at the end of the eighteenth century are tremendous feats of engineering. They are even more impressive when you remember that there were no giant earth-moving

machines, no reinforced concrete, and no huge lorries to take away the earth dug out from the site of the lock.

For example, the Caen Hill Locks outside Devizes in Wiltshire, on the Kennet and Avon Canal, raise the canal 70 metres by means of 29 locks – 15 of them in a straight line one after the other. It was a great feat of engineering skill – and a great test of the boat people's strength and stamina.

BUILDING A LOCK

In contrast to the rather leisurely scene opposite, this hive of activity shows a lock being built, 1910. The building equipment has probably changed little from when the series of Caen Hill Locks (see opposite) were finished a century earlier, although the wheelbarrows then may have had wooden rather than metal wheels!

The very first lock in England was constructed on the Exeter Canal, built in 1564-6 as a link between Exeter and Countess Wear. Many of the early locks had sides covered in turf, but these did not last very long. They were soon replaced with walls of wood, stone or, as here, bricks.

The walls needed to be strong because of the changes of pressure against them. This varied according to whether the sluices in the upper gate were open to let water in and so raise the level of the water in the lock, or whether it was the sluices in the lower gate that were open to let water out and thus lower the level of water in the lock. In general, a lock raised or lowered a boat by between 2 and 3 metres.

The photograph shows how thick the walls will be when the lock chamber is finished. Judging by the depth of the lock opposite, these bricklayers have nearly reached the top of the wall. That is why wooden platforms have been built up for them to stand on – there was no tubular steel scaffolding then! And what do you think the slide is for?

Some say that the men who built the canals stayed on to become the boatmen. But if this ever was the case, and there are many who doubt it, it was certainly not so for the men in this photograph. They are firmly land-based bricklayers, and when this lock is finished they will probably be at work building houses or factories.

A CHRISTENING

You might think that these canal women are going to a funeral in their dark clothes and elaborate black bonnets. But in fact this is a christening party, photographed in 1913. The group are posed on the roof and around the entrance to the cabin of a narrow boat. They probably did not all live on this boat, but all the same you can see just how tiny the living quarters were.

Beyond the cabin is the cargo area. Notice how the protective canvas covers are partly pulled up and held in place by ropes. These are attached to the boards that run above the centre of the cargo hold.

This boat is horse-drawn, not a steamer like the one on page 22. The chimney beside which the small child is sitting comes from the stove in the cabin below. Imagine having to cook for a whole family in such cramped quarters. (For a photograph of the inside of a cabin, turn to page 34.)

Is the child a boy or girl? The cap suggests a boy, but the white collar and apron seem to indicate a girl. Don't forget, though, that it was quite usual for the children of poor families – and the boat people were poor – to wear the clothes of their

CANAL CHILDREN

(Above) It's just an ordinary working day for these boat children, although having their photograph taken probably makes it a little special. And what a working day it would be, too – not behind school desks but on the boat, helping to earn the family's living.

Providing an education for boat children was a problem. In the early days of the canals, most of the boatmen lived on land. They went only on regular runs lasting a few days, and worked their boat with the help of a hired hand. And, of course, in those days at the end of the eighteenth and the beginning of the nineteenth centuries, education for children was not considered important.

Later, as the railways became an increasing threat to the canals, the boat people were forced to give up their homes on land and they moved onto the boats – into the tiny cabins you can see on these two boats.

There was no longer any paid help, either. The boatman's wife and children had to help at the locks, look after the horse and, where necessary, leg the boat through tunnels (see page 37). As they were always on the move, it was almost impossible for the children to go to school.

At the beginning of the nineteenth century a number of charities tried to set up schools – and particularly Sunday schools – for these children. But most of such well-meaning efforts were short lived. The Canal Boat Acts of 1877 and 1884, which contained special arrangements for educating children, were equally unsuccessful.

Like their parents and grandparents, the eight children in the photograph – there are two with the boat woman – probably could not read or write. But, as one NSPCC inspector said, they are sharp in many other ways, and 'you needn't teach them a thing about money'.

older brothers and sisters regardless of sex. And if you think the child's heavy boots might be a clue, take a look at the boots of the couple (the baby's parents?) sitting on the cabin roof.

A HARD LIFE

If you ever thought that living and working on the canals must have been a pleasant, rather romantic way of life, have a look at the couple in this picture. Their appearance speaks all too clearly of a life of hard work and few comforts.

By the 1920s, when this photograph was taken, the canals were really in decline. Competition from the railways had become tougher as the years went by, and the only way the canals could compete was by cutting their charges for carrying goods until there was almost no profit. And if there was little profit, there was little with which to pay the boatmen.

Compare the state of this boat with the ones on pages 22 and 23. The watercans may still have a trace of their old decoration, but if they do it's hidden under rust and dirt.

Gone, too, are any signs of the canal people's distinctive clothes. In their place sacking provides some extra warmth over ragged clothes worn thin with age and repeated washing.

Only the little dog, and the canary in its cage between the watercans and the bucket, are reminders of once better days.

JAZZ PARTY

What a contrast between this photograph and the one opposite. At a jazz party beside the River Thames in 1924, the 'bright young things', the trend-setters of the time, enjoy themselves trying out the steps of the latest dances to the music of 'The Monte Carlo Bandits'. In the background a pleasure steamer goes by. There is no hint here that the country's waterways provide both homes and a hard living for many people.

It must be a warm summer's day,

because some of the girls are wearing only bathing costumes with their high heels and cloche hats – these bathing costumes are rather more covered up than the ones we're used to today.

As cars became cheaper, many beauty spots in the country and at the riverside were developed into fashionable places to visit for a meal or a night out. Restaurants like this one, with their own dance floors and bands, were especially popular.

The man on the left looks as if he just can't wait to have a turn on the floor. Notice his white flannels, blazer, and collar and tie. These may not be jeans and a tee-shirt, but they were their equivalents in the 1920s.

MOONLIGHT

Not many landsmen ever get this view of their towns and cities, but for the people who lived and worked on the waterways it was quite usual. In fact, for them, it was the city streets that provided the unusual view.

It is a fairly clear night, and the moonlight is reflected in the windows of the lockkeepers' cottages and the waters of the canal. Tied up alongside are two large craft, probably the local Mersey flats. Further down the canal the moonlight shows a narrow boat slowly approaching.

The factory chimneys in the background of the photograph are a reminder that the boat people did not only work in country areas. These are the Hulme Locks on the Bridgewater Canal at the point where it joins the Rochdale Canal.

The construction of the Bridgewater Canal started the great canal-building boom at the end of the eighteenth century – a boom that is sometimes referred to as 'canal

mania' – when people realized just how useful, and profitable, canals could be.

The men who designed the Duke of Bridgewater's canal, John Gilbert and James Brindley, also developed the narrow boats that worked on the smaller waterways. These boats were based on the long thin boats, nicknamed 'starvationers' because you could see their ribs, that were used at the duke's coalmines.

The narrow boats varied from

WAREHOUSE FIRE

(Above) With all the water close by, a riverside fire should be easy to deal with! But, of course, it's not as simple as that, because warehouses often hold large quantities of highly inflammable material.

When a tea warehouse at Colonial Wharf, Wapping, in East London, caught fire in September 1935, the blaze was so great that the whole area of the docks was threatened. The fire quickly spread to a neighbouring rubber warehouse, and the resulting thick black acrid smoke was an extra hazard for the firemen.

While fire brigades from the surrounding area were called in to fight the fire from the land, fire floats fought the blaze from the river. Even though the fire float cannot get right alongside – you can see other boats moored at the dockside – the powerful jets from the fire hoses still reach to the densest, blackest smoke, the seat of the fire.

The smoke was so thick that many of the firemen fighting this blaze from the land had to wear gas masks, although the men on the fire float are not.

Sadly, only four years later, gas masks became part of all firemen's equipment, and soon afterwards dock fires were an almost daily occurrence. Why? With the start of the Second World War (1939-45), the docks were a prime target for the enemy's bombs.

canal to canal, but most were about 21.9 metres long and 1.9 metres wide, only very slightly smaller than the locks through which they had to pass (page 24). The early narrow boats carried cargoes of about 20 to 30 tonnes. The barges and flats were, of course, much larger and could carry more, but there were fewer waterways on which they could work.

FATHER CHRISTMAS

It's Christmas 1937, and Father Christmas is doing his rounds. He's actually Mr Wall of the Canal Boatmen's Institute, but never mind, it's a great treat!

The welfare of the canal people, and especially the children, had worried well-intentioned people ever since the first canals were built. In general, efforts to express that concern in a practical way came to nothing, largely because they met with hostility from the boat people, who feared and resented what they saw as interference by people 'from the land'.

One of the most successful of the welfare societies was the Canalmen and Boatmen's Friend Society. The missionaries employed by the society made regular visits to the boats, writing letters, helping with family problems, explaining any new regulations and, most important of all, just chatting and being friendly with everyone.

But there still remained the problem of the children on the boats. Work on the boats was hard and it had to be done whatever the weather. Long after Parliament had passed acts preventing children from working in mines and factories, boat children were working as hard as ever in conditions that were just as tough.

The NSPCC (National Society for the Prevention of Cruelty to Children) was particularly concerned about the children, knowing the accidents and injuries that could all too easily happen. In 1919 a Canal Boats Inspector was appointed to ensure that children were not made to do unsuitable work.

Even if the inspector seldom caught anyone, sympathetic lockkeepers could now say to a boatman, 'The Children's Inspector is around', and immediately the child would be given an easier task.

PETROL SHORTAGE

(Right) The Second World War (1939-45) brought many shortages and restrictions. Food and clothing were rationed and so was petrol. As a result, the rivers came into their own during the war, at least for short journeys.

Here at Windsor in Berkshire, the boatmen are doing good business, despite the cold and dreary day. But with a war on and petrol rationed, you'd probably never have guessed that they are taking their passengers to the races!

LONDON-ON-SEA

(Below) The sand and water may be a little dirty, but it's better than nothing. Here, just below Tower Bridge, families from all over the City and East End of London throng the 'beach'.

There's swimming and paddling – someone has even got the inner tube from a tyre to help a nervous swimmer.

There's a deckchair man too, so you don't have to sit on hard, wet sand. And waves? Well, the passing boats make those!

THE END OF AN ERA

These three photographs, taken in the 1950s, record a way of life that was fast disappearing then, and today has really gone.

Look carefully at the picture of the narrow boat's cabin (left). This is no museum reconstruction, but the way generations of canal people had lived. The oil lamp gleams, and there are cooking pans and a handsome copper kettle on the tiny stove – you can see the chimney from a stove such as this in the picture on the right. The lattice edges to the plates echo the crochet runners on the shelves and the fringing on the curtain pelmet.

The cupboard beside the stove in the picture on the left is decorated with the same traditional motifs as the boat on the right (top): Mrs Evans's boat *Snowflake* has particularly fine castle views, both on the cabin doors and on the large panel beside the company's nameboard. But such painting, exposed as it is to all weathers, needs looking after, and you can see how it's beginning to flake and wear around the edges of the nameboards.

The old lady (right), with her jug of flowers, wears a boat woman's traditional bonnet, though it's white and much smaller than the black ones worn by the canal women on pages 26 and 27. But the photo shows clearly how they were made. The heavily stitched brim helped to shade the eyes, while the 'curtain' at the back kept the sun and rain off the back of the wearer's neck.

Notice that there are no ribbons or strings to tie the bonnet on with. Ribbons and strings could come undone, and probably at an awkward moment. These bonnets fitted close to the head, like a hat, staying firmly in place in wind and rain.

The old lady looks back on a life Mrs Evans's little boy will probably never know. On most canals today, the only boats are pleasure boats used by holidaymakers.

1950s

The photographs on the right and at the top of the page opposite, both taken in the 1950s, show aspects of a canalman's work that had almost disappeared. The bottom picture opposite shows why.

HORSE-DRAWN BARGE

Scenes like this one had been typical of canals for almost 200 years. The clothes of the canal people varied, and the goods their boats carried could change, but there was always the same broad towpath, beaten flat by horses' hooves as they drew the laden boats along at a steady, gentle pace.

Horses had pulled canal boats since the first canals came into operation. Occasionally mules were used instead and there were also a few sailing barges, but horses were the usual source of power for the canal boats.

With the development of engines some companies introduced 'steamers', barges with steam-powered engines (see page 22), but horses still pulled most boats. This was not as odd or old-fashioned of the canal people as you might think. Steam-driven boats were only economical if they could go fast, or if a big company could afford a large number to tow other barges.

Most of Britain's canals were too narrow and had too many locks for the steamers to go much faster than the horse-drawn boats, and most canal boat operators were too small to have a fleet of steamers like Fellows, Morton & Clayton (see page 23).

But as steam and later diesel engines became smaller and more efficient, and the competition from the railways fiercer, horse-drawn canal boats gradually disappeared. This photograph shows the last horse-drawn boat on the Leeds and Liverpool Canal.

LEGGING

Legging was probably the hardest thing a canalman had to do. A horse could not pull a boat through a tunnel – constructing tunnels had been difficult enough for the early canal engineers without providing a towpath as well. Instead, the boatmen had to walk – or 'leg' – the boat through the tunnels. The two men here are using the sides of the tunnel, but sometimes they would lie on the top plank above the cargo and 'leg' along the tunnel roof.

This boat has a powerful lamp mounted on its bow but, in the early days of canals, legging was done in the dark or with only a flickering lantern to light the tunnel's gloom.

Legging, of course, was unnecessary on steamers or other self-propelled boats – a great improvement for the boatmen!

MOTOR CANAL BOATS

Motor-driven canal boats, which could carry cargo and pull another boat laden with cargo, gradually replaced the horse-drawn boats.

After the Second World War, the canals were nationalized by the government and the British Waterways Board was set up. You can see that this narrow boat, photographed in 1955 on the Oxford Canal near Rugby, has 'British Waterways 232' painted on its side. It is registered at Brentford in West London.

The photograph shows how much some things on the canals had changed. The towpath, for instance, is overgrown because it is no longer used by horses many times a day. And there are bicycles propped against the cargo. But notice the links with early photographs in this book. There are rose and castle designs around the cabin door. The tiller bar is striped, and the cargo is coal, and there are still planks along the top over which tarpaulins can be thrown in bad weather.

The photographs here illustrate two uses of rivers not mentioned so far in this book: for the supply of water and of power.

RESERVOIR

The dramatic photograph opposite shows the Penygarreg Dam and Reservoir in the Elan Valley in Powys, Wales. The huge lake in the background was formed when the valley was dammed and flooded in 1952 as part of a scheme to ensure an adequate supply of water to Birmingham and other places in the Midlands of Britain.

The reservoir covers many square miles, and though the area was thinly populated, some people had to be moved to new homes as the water covered their old ones.

Have you noticed the road on the left of the picture? It's not completely level as it winds around the hillside, but notice how close it is to the reservoir in the background and how far from the little river in the foreground of the photograph. This gives a very clear indication of how huge the reservoir is and just how high up the hillside its waters now lap.

The still waters of the reservoir end abruptly as water cascades in a white sheet over the dam wall and into the original river valley. The style of the little building on the wall is in marked contrast to the square, blocky architecture of the power station on the right.

HYDRO-ELECTRIC DAM

The Pitlochry Dam (above) in Perthshire, Scotland, may not be as decorative as the Penygarreg Dam (opposite), but it, too, controls a river to provide an essential twentieth-century resource: hydro-electricity.

This Scottish valley had a dam built across it. Behind the dam a lake formed, just as it did in the Elan Valley. Water from the lake is used to turn turbines. As the turbines turn, they generate electricity.

Hydro-electric plants need a constant flow of water. This is why the Pitlochry Dam was built – to create a reservoir to control and even out the flow of water to the turbines. There are sluices at the top of the dam to control the amount of water in the reservoir.

Dams are designed to hold back a certain quantity of water and can give way if too much water collects in the reservoir behind them. The water you can see flowing down the sloping wall of the dam is part of this safety system. To turn the turbines and generate electricity a great deal of water has to fall from quite a height.

ABANDONED DEPOT

(Right) It wasn't only the waterways that suffered neglect as canal businesses declined and died. The buildings of the once bustling canal depots and 'ports' also fell derelict.

You'd never guess from this photograph of it taken in 1968, but one of the biggest and most important of these ports was Netherpool which, in 1797, was renamed Ellesmere Port. Situated on the Shropshire Union Canal, it was an important centre for the transfer of goods from sea-going vessels to river and canal boats (and vice versa).

The warehouses in this photograph were designed by the famous Scottish engineer Thomas Telford (1757-1834) who also designed the Caledonian Canal (page 21), the Pontcysyllte Aqueduct (page 42), and the great suspension bridge that spans the Menai Straits between Wales and the island of Anglesey.

Sadly these fine warehouses no longer exist. Severely damaged by fire, they had to be pulled down.

NEGLECT

(Left) The Kennet and Avon Canal opened in 1810. It linked the rivers Avon and Thames, so that boats could now go from the English Channel in the east to the Bristol Channel in the west entirely by river and canal – a much safer and quicker route than by sea. The canal included the great flight of locks at Caen Hill (page 24).

Sadly, this photograph, taken early in the 1960s at Bathford in Somerset, gives few clues to the canal's better days. The sluggish water, seldom stirred now by the passage of boats, has enabled plants to grow thickly along the banks and even encroach into the water, narrowing the canal. The surface of the water has large patches of waterweed on it. And the towpath has become a winding path for walkers and holidaymakers to stroll along.

VOLUNTEERS AT WORK

(Above) The other two pictures shown here tell a sad tale, of the neglect of a once proud industry. But times change, and attitudes often change with them. That has certainly been the case with canals. Although the last cargo-carrying company went out of business in 1970, the long years of decline on many canals is over.

This photograph would have been impossible to take in the 1950s. In fact people then would have found it hard to imagine anyone spending their free time in mud and water rebuilding, restoring and generally reviving neglected canals. But that is what is happening.

Although the canals may never again carry goods traffic, they have a promising future for leisure activities. It will be a long time before this stretch of the Kennet and Avon Canal takes a boat, but these are two of the many enthusiastic volunteers all over the country who are ensuring that canals will have some sort of future.

A ROVING BRIDGE

(Above) Compared with the obvious technical brilliance of Telford's Pontcysyllte Aqueduct (right), this little bridge over the Macclesfield Canal may seem rather unimpressive. But it, too, is an example of the careful design and building that mark many canals.

Towpaths did not always run on the same side of a canal. Perhaps there was a natural obstacle, or a landowner didn't want to lose land to the towpath. When this happened a bridge had to be built so that the canal horses could cross to the other bank. Generally the bridge was a curved one, known as a roving bridge. These bridges avoided the need to unhitch the horse from the boat (which wasted time) because the towpath was continuous. The horse just went up over the bridge and down under the bridge on the other bank. See if you can work out how!

Look at the stonework of the bridge, especially where it curves, and at the beautifully shaped parapet stones. And have you noticed that the cobbled towpath is much lower in the middle where, in the days before motor boats, the hooves of hundreds of horses wore it down?

AN AQUEDUCT

(Right) This is not a railway bridge – it is the Pontcysyllte Aqueduct which carries the Llangollen Canal over the River Dee near Llangollen in Wales.

If you think it looks high it is – 36 metres. But what you can't see from the photograph is its length – 307 metres. Of all the many great engineering feats achieved by the early canal builders, this is one of the finest. It was designed by Thomas Telford (see also page 40), and was opened in 1805.

Aqueducts were nothing new, of course. The Romans built many in their empire over 2,000 years ago. But Telford's idea was revolutionary. He used stone columns to support what is really a huge iron trough containing the canal. The design was so successful that it was later copied by the railway engineers.

The fact that the aqueduct is still in use more than 180 years later shows both Telford's brilliance as an engineer and the skill of the men who built it.

A CHANGELESS SCENE?

(Right) This view of the Napton flight of locks on the Oxford Canal was taken from the top of Napton Hill, looking towards the Thames Valley. It seems to show a scene of the typical, timeless British countryside. Or does it?

That question should not really surprise you. After all, canals are artificial, man-made things, just as railways and roads are. It's hard to imagine now, but at the end of the eighteenth century, Britain's countryside was as scarred by earthworks, building contractors and large numbers of men at work as any motorway site today. The population of Britain was smaller then, and many of the canals crossed rural areas, so fewer people were disrupted by the building of canals than by today's motorways. But, on the other hand, there were no huge excavators or other pieces of equipment, so canal building was a very slow process.

Next time you stop to admire a view of the countryside, look a little harder at it. There may not be a canal, but you may spot a nice wide straight track between high hedges. That'll be the remains of a railway line – another change in the changeless landscape!

43

1980s

BINGLEY FIVE RISE

This photograh of the flight of locks at Bingley, known as the Bingley Five Rise, on the Leeds and Liverpool Canal, shows very clearly how canal engineers coped when land levels changed. Each of these five locks lowers (or raises) a boat 3.6 metres, so in a distance of less than 120 metres the level of the canal changes by 18 metres.

The very first canals followed the contours of the landscape. Their courses were carefully plotted to avoid natural obstacles. This often meant the canals followed rather long routes. As competition between the canal companies increased, shorter and therefore quicker routes were sought.

Caen Hill (page 24), Pontcysyllte (page 42) and Bingley Five Rise are just three of the feats of canal engineering that survive as monuments to the men who designed, financed, built and worked the first efficient system of long-distance transport this country had known.

INQUISITIVE SPECTATORS

Messing about in boats can be immense fun. It can also be enormously embarrassing!

1564 Construction of the Exeter Canal linking Exeter and Countess Wear. Includes the first-known locks in Britain

1721 Rivers Irwell and Mersey made navigable to help trade with Manchester. Work was completed by 1736

1727 *Sensitivity of silver salts to light discovered*

1742 The Newry Canal in Northern Ireland opens to carry coal from Tyrone to the port of Newry

1761 Bridgewater Canal opens

1772 Regular passenger services start on the Bridgewater Canal from Liverpool to Warrington

1787 'The Trial', probably Britain's first iron barge, launched on the River Severn at Coalbrookdale

1797 Netherpool on the Wirral Peninsula is renamed Ellesmere Port

1800 *Tom Wedgwood makes 'sun' pictures by placing leaves on specially treated leather and leaving them in the sun. The parts covered by the leaves did not darken like the rest, and when the leaves were removed, their image remained on the leather*

1803 Building of the Caledonian Canal begins to provide a quick passage from the east to the west coast of Scotland in time of war

1805 Telford's Pontcysyllte Aqueduct on the Llangollen Canal opens

1810 The Kennet and Avon Canal opens, providing a direct inland shipping route from the east to west coasts of Britain

1817 Regent's Canal and the Gloucester and Berkeley (now the Gloucester and Sharpness Ship) Canal are completed

1825 The Stockton and Darlington Railway opens The fastest boats take three days to travel the 93 miles from Birmingham to Preston Brook where the Trent and Mersey meets the Birmingham Canal

1830 Liverpool and Manchester Railway opens

1840 The peak of the canal age – 6,576 km of canal are open

1846 Railway promoters get permission from Parliament to build over 6,000 km of railway line. Similar permission was granted in following years

1855 *Roger Fenton takes documentary photographs of the Crimean War*

1877 Canal Boats Act attempts to regulate living conditions on board canal boats

1888 *The first Kodak camera is produced Kodak film processing service is set up by George Eastman*

1892 *Cine film is perfected*

1894 Opening of the Manchester Ship Canal Tolls and other charges on canals regulated by Parliament

1907 *Autochrome, the first practical system of colour photography, goes on sale*

1909 Royal Commission on Canals and Inland Navigation recommends nationalization of main waterway routes, and standardization of the sizes of boats

1914 First World War begins

1918 First World War ends

1929 *Flashbulbs for cameras are introduced, enabling pictures to be taken in bad light*

1935 *Kodachrome, the first modern film, goes on sale. In an improved version it is still used for slides*

1939 Second World War begins

1945 Second World War ends

1947 *'Instant' Polaroid cameras go on sale*

1948 Waterways are nationalized

1959 First section of the M1 motorway opens

1963 *Polaroid colour cameras go on sale Kodak introduce the first 'Instamatic' camera* British Waterways Board formed to oversee the country's waterways

1969 *First photographs taken on the moon*

1970 Last cargo-carrying company on the canals goes out of business

1978 Members of two job creation schemes clear and restore stretches of the Kennet and Avon Canal

The entries in *italics* refer to developments in photography

Things to do

YOUR LOCAL WATERWAY

What is your nearest waterway? (If you think it is some way away, you may be in for a surprise. After all, the country has a good many rivers, and with over 6,500 km of canals at one time there was probably once a waterway nearer you than you think.) Check with your local library and then write its history.

Here are some ideas on the sort of information to include: when and why was it built (if it is, or was, a canal), where does it run from and to, what were the principal cargoes that were carried along it, what sort of boats used it, were there any obstacles or great engineering works along its course, such as locks, bridges, shallows or ferry crossings?

If the waterway no longer exists or is not used for cargo, explain why. Did roads and railways provide a more efficient form of transport? Or perhaps the goods carried were no longer required? This happened quite often when, for example, a factory stopped using coal to power its machines and used oil instead.

TYPES OF BOAT

There was enormous variety in the types of boat that sailed on Britain's waterways.

Find out about as many as possible of the different types of boat, and then describe one or two of them in detail – perhaps the ones used in your area.

Illustrate your descriptions with plans and drawings of the boats, and mention any adaptations that came, for example, with the change to using engines instead of horses or sails.

WORKING ON THE WATER

The waterways provided many different types of job. As well as the people who worked the boats, there were lock-keepers, warehouse-men, clerks who checked the goods, others who collected the tolls that had to be paid for using the canals, and, of course, the canal-builders.

Choose one of these groups of people and find out all you can about the work they did and the lives they led, and what a typical working day was like.

Women rarely worked on the waterways, except to help their husbands, and at least one canal boat company prohibited women on its boats. But there are records of the widows of canal boatmen continuing to run the boat after their husbands' deaths. If you describe a day in the life of a canal boat woman, don't forget that she'll have the family to feed as well doing the work needed on the boat.

A CARGO'S JOURNEY

Many canals were built and rivers improved to provide better transport for a particular cargo: salt from Cheshire, building stone from the Peak District, roofing slate from Wales, and coal from many different areas.

Choose one type of cargo and follow its journey from mine or quarry down the canals or rivers to its destination. What happened to it once it was unloaded? What was it used for, and is it still used for this purpose or has some modern synthetic product superseded it?

PHOTO ALBUM

Scenes with water in them often make rather special photographs, so why not try a photographic record of your local waterway?

Obviously this is quite easy if it still exists or you live quite near it. But even if the waterway has long since silted up, you'd be surprised how many traces it may have left. Did it have locks? If so, are the lock-keepers' cottages still there? Sometimes you may even find a small bridge standing apparently in the middle of nowhere. Look at it carefully – it may have a metal plate with the name or initials of the company which built it. (You can see a plate with a number on it in the photo of the roving bridge on page 42.)

CANAL RESCUE

Throughout the country there are many local groups of enthusiasts who are helping to restore and re-build old and neglected waterways (see page 41). Your library may be able to tell you if there's such a group in your area and give you the name of the local organizer. If not, write to the:

British Waterways Board,
Melbury House,
Melbury Terrace,
London, NW1.

They will be able to give you the information you need. The work can be great fun, and it isn't all standing about in mud. Towpaths have to be cleared and kept clear, for example. And if you have helped to restore a waterway, what could be more satisfying than to travel by boat along it when the work is done?

Narrow boats at work by Michael E. Ware (Moorland Publishing)

A fascinating collection of photographs from the last century to the 1960s which fully lives up to the title of the book. As well as the boats and the people who worked them, the photographs show the places where they worked – the wharfs and quays, the warehouses and locks – and the types of cargo carried. The extensive captions to the pictures are particularly interesting and informative.

The canal age by Charles Hadfield (David and Charles)

The story of the canals from their very earliest days to the 1970s. The author covers all aspects: how canals were planned, who financed them, who designed and built them, and the work of all those involved with them, both on the boats and on shore. The book also includes chapters on canals in North America and Europe which provide an interesting comparison to British ones.

Britain's canal and river craft by E. Paget-Tomlinson (Moorland Publishing)

A comprehensive study of all the many types of boat that were used on Britain's waterways – and there was a tremendous variety! As well as a detailed and slightly technical text, the book includes line drawings of the different types of boat and early photographs of many of them.

Canal people by Harry Hanson (David and Charles)

Concentrating almost entirely on the people who worked on the boats on Britain's waterways from the 1760s to the 1970s, the author uses many contemporary sources of information. The extensive quotations show very clearly just what a hard life the canal people had.

William Jessop, engineer by Charles Hadfield and A. W. Skempton (David and Charles)

A very readable biography of one of the greatest engineers of the canal age, who also played an important part in the development of London docks and was a pioneer railway builder.

Narrow boat painting by A. J. Lewery (David and Charles)

Canal boats are well-known for their decorations, particularly the traditional 'roses and castles' designs. The author traces the history and development of these and other patterns which the canal people used to brighten their tiny cabin homes.

Britain's lost waterways Volume 1 Inland navigations by Michael E. Ware (Moorland Publishing)
Britain's lost waterways Volume 2 Navigations to the sea by Michael E. Ware (Moorland Publishing)

Two collections of wonderfully nostalgic old photographs that in some ways are rather sad. They give an excellent idea of the size and scope of water-borne traffic in this country. Many of the canals that made this possible have now almost completely disappeared.

Backdoor Britain by Anthony Burton (Magnum)

An account, by an unashamed canal enthusiast, of a trip he took in 1975 around the still navigable canals of Britain.

Canals and rivers of Britain by Andrew Darwin (Dent)

An illustrated guide and survey of the country's canals as they are today. The author gives a brief survey of each one's history and then gives information about boating on them today.

For more detailed accounts of the canals of individual areas of the country, both David and Charles and Moorland Publishing produce excellent books on specific areas.

The former company publishes these books under the series title of 'Canals of the British Isles'.

Your local library and county records office are probably good sources of local information, and may even have published a booklet about your area which includes information about canals. Many libraries also have collections of old photographs which you can see on request.

Index